West Chicago Public Library District
118 West Washington
West Chicago, IL 60185-2803
Phone # (630) 231-1552

Structural Wonders

Sears Tower

Lauren Diemer

Weigl Publishers Inc.

Published by Weigl Publishers Inc.
350 5th Avenue, Suite 3304, PMB 6G
New York, NY 10118-0069

Website: www.weigl.com

Library of Congress Cataloging-in-Publication Data

Diemer, Lauren.
  Sears Tower : structural wonders / Lauren Diemer.
      p. cm. -- (Structural wonders)
  Includes index.
  ISBN 978-1-60596-138-5 (hard cover : alk. paper) --
  ISBN 978-1-60596-139-2 (soft cover : alk. paper)
  1. Sears Tower (Chicago, Ill.)--Juvenile literature.
  2. Skyscrapers--Illinois--Chicago--Design and construction--Juvenile literature.
  3. Chicago (Ill.)--Buildings, structures, etc.--Juvenile literature. I. Title.
  NA6233.C4S432 2009
  720'.4830977311--dc22
                              2009004988

Printed in China
1 2 3 4 5 6 7 8 9 0 13 12 11 10 09

Photograph Credits
Every reasonable effort has been made to trace ownership and to obtain
permission to reprint copyright material. The publishers would be pleased
to have any errors or omissions brought to their attention so that they may
be corrected in subsequent printings.

Weigl acknowledges Getty Images as its primary image supplier for this title.

All of the internet URLs given in the book were valid at the time of publication.
However, due to the dynamic nature of the Internet, some addresses may have
changed, or sites may have ceased to exist since publication. While the author
and publisher regret any inconvenience this may cause readers, no responsibility
for any such changes can be accepted by either the author or the publisher.

Project Coordinators: Heather C. Hudak, Heather Kissock
Design: Terry Paulhus

Contents

What is the Sears Tower?

The Sears Tower rises majestically above the Chicago skyline. At 1450 feet (442 meters), it was once the tallest building in the world. Since its completion in 1973, other buildings have surpassed this height, but the Sears Tower is still one of the five tallest buildings in the world.

The Sears Tower is a skyscraper. This means it is a tall building in which people live or work. Skyscrapers stand taller than the other buildings in a city. There is no height requirement for a building to be called a skyscraper. It only has to rise above the rest of the city's skyline.

The Sears Tower's design concept was unique for its time. The building consists of nine large square tubes placed together. All of the tubes are present at the base of the building. However, while some of the tubes extend the entire height of the building, others stop much earlier. This design gives the building its stepped appearance and provides the lower levels with more office space.

This unique and useful design was the idea of an **architect** named Bruce Graham. He was hired by the department store Sears Roebuck and Company to create a building that could serve as the company's main office. The large office space in the lower levels were designed with them in mind. The smaller offices at the higher levels of the building were to be rented to other companies.

Sears stayed in the building for about 20 years. Then, in 1992, they sold their part of the building and eventually moved to another location. Until 2009, the name remained as a tribute to the company that built the skyscraper. At that time, the building was renamed Willis Tower in honor of its main tenants.

Quick Bites

- During construction, it took workers too long to climb down for meals. Special kitchens where workers could eat were created on two floors halfway up the tower.
- The word "skyscraper" originated at sea. It the name sailors gave to the mast of their ships.
- The Sears Tower has 110 **stories**.

Building History

When Sears Roebuck first hatched the idea of building a **landmark** skyscraper as its head office, the company was at the peak of its success. It was the world's largest retailer, with operations in more than 13 countries, a large catalog ordering business, and an annual income of about $450 million. It wanted a building that would demonstrate the size and success of the company. The head office alone had to house about 13,000 employees.

Plans for the building were much smaller in scale at first. It was to be a big, box-like building meant to house only the Sears employees. However, the company's advisors believed that a larger building would be more suitable for a growing company. They suggested that the building house not only the Sears head office, but other office space as well. This space could be rented to other companies until Sears needed it.

The outside of the tower has been climbed twice. Dan Goodwin climbed it in 1981 and Alain Robert in 1999.

The size of the proposed building increased a great deal due to this idea. Originally meant to cover 3 million square feet (278,709 square meters), the building was redesigned to cover 4.5 million square feet (418,064 sq m) and have 110 stories. Its planned height of 1,450 feet (442 m) was taller than the World Trade Towers in New York.

On a clear day, you can see four states from the Sears Tower Visitor Skydeck—Illinois, Indiana, Michigan, and Wisconsin.

1969: Sears Roebuck purchases 3 acres (0.01 square kilometers) of land in downtown Chicago for its new head office.

July 1970: The building's design is unveiled.

August 1970: The building's **groundbreaking ceremony** is held.

June 1971: Construction of the tower's steel frame begins.

May 1973: The building's final steel beam is placed in a **topping out ceremony**.

1974: Construction of the Sears Tower is completed.

February 1982: Antennas are added to the building, increasing its height to 1,707 feet (527.3 m).

1992: Sears Roebuck moves out of the Sears Tower.

June 2000: One of the antennas is extended, bringing the tower's height to 1,730 feet (527 m).

Commonly, modern buildings are built using materials such as concrete, glass, and steel.

Sometimes, the wind blew so hard workers could not stand up. This would postpone construction for the day.

At the time, they were the tallest buildings in the world. This led Sears to proclaim their intention to make their head office the world's tallest building.

The job of making this goal a reality was given to the architectural firm of Skidmore, Owings, and Merrill, based in Chicago. The architect in charge was Bruce Graham, and the chief **structural engineer** was Fazlur Khan. Together, they drew up the plans to create a unique structure that reflected the success of its owners.

Construction on the Sears Tower began in August, 1970. Its final **beam** was placed on May 3, 1973. The structure was completed the following year.

Overlooking the Chicago skyline, the Sears Tower is an example of modern style. This means it has a simple design rejecting all decoration.

Big Ideas

When Bruce Graham created the design of the Sears Tower, he planned a skyscraper with a square, stepped appearance. This building style was innovative, eye-catching, and unlike any other structure that had ever been built. The job of creating the pieces that would make up the building fell to the structural engineer, Fazlur Khan.

It was Khan's idea to use the "bundled tubes" that make up the building's steps. Each tube has a framework of steel beams and **columns**. When grouped together, this framework gives the building support. The Sears Tower is made up of nine tubes. All tubes are present at the base of the tower, with some ending before reaching the top of the building. Each tube works together with its neighboring tubes to resist outside forces, such as gravity and wind.

As Chicago is often called the "Windy City," it was important that the tower be built to withstand high winds. Even though Chicago's wind speed averages at 10.4 miles (16.7 km) per hour, winds can gust to speeds up to 57 miles (92 km) per hour. Fazlur Khan's job was to build the tower in such a way that it would not sway very much under these forces. In using the bundled tubes, he succeeded. The building has an average sway of only 6 inches (15.2 centimeters) from the center.

Web Link:
To learn more about bundled tube construction, go to www.allaboutskyscrapers.com/ sp.sears_tower.htm

1) The antennas on the Sears tower are struck by lightening about 660 times per year. 2) The antennas change color based on the holiday. 3) The 103th floor observation Skydeck offers views spanning 50 miles (80.5 km).

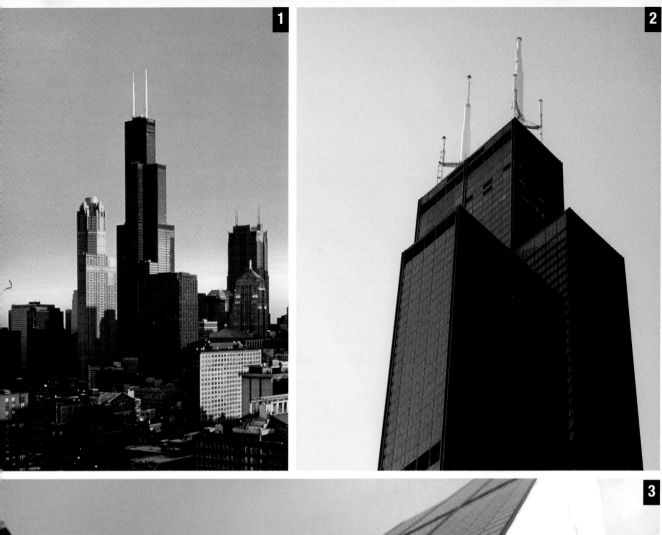

Sears Tower

Profile:
Bruce Graham, Architect

Bruce Graham, the architect of the Sears Tower, was born in Bogota, Colombia, in 1925, to American parents. As a young adult, he attended the University of Dayton and the Case School of Applied Sciences, in Cleveland. When World War II broke out, he joined the Navy. Following the war, he returned to his education at Case School. In 1948, he graduated from the University of Pennsylvania with a bachelor's degree in architecture. Following graduation, he accepted a position at the architectural firm of Holabird, Root, and Burgee.

Bruce proved to be a talented architect. After only three years with Holabird, Root, and Burgee, he left the company to become the chief of design at the Chicago firm of Skidmore, Owings, and Merrill. He was promoted to partner in 1960. Bruce specialized in designing corporate high-rises. His buildings can be found throughout Chicago and in many parts of the world.

Bruce's designs were heavily influenced by the works of another well-known architect by the name of Ludwig Mies Van der Rohe. Van der Rohe believed in simple designs for buildings. His buildings are characterized by open spaces and minimal framework. This "less is more" attitude can be seen in Bruce Graham's design of the Sears Tower, as well as his other buildings.

THE WORK OF BRUCE GRAHAM

John Hancock Center, Chicago, Illinois (1970)
Known for the criss-cross beams running across its **facade,** the John Hancock Center is a well-known Chicago skyscraper. Inside its 100 stories are retail shops, restaurants, apartment condominiums, and offices. The building is known for its tapering lines. This means that it is broad at the bottom and narrow at the top.

Inland Steel Building, Chicago, Illinois (1957)
Chicago's Inland Steel Building was one of the first skyscrapers to be built downtown after the Great Depression. Appropriately, the building features stainless steel **cladding**, in honor of the company that resides in it. In 1998, the Inland Steel Building was given official landmark designation by the city of Chicago.

Originally, the Sears Tower was supposed to be two shorter twin towers.

Bruce remained at Skidmore, Owings, and Merrill until 1989. He then moved to Hobe Sound, Florida, with his wife. There, the two of them formed their own architectural firm called Graham and Graham, which remains active to this day.

Over the course of his career, Bruce has received many honors and awards. He has served on many architectural and urban planning boards. He is a trustee of the University of Pennsylvania and an honorary member of the Royal Institute of British Architects.

Bruce Graham has always believed that working architects should teach architecture. As a result, he has taught architecture to students at Harvard University. In his personal life, his interests are centered on the arts, philosophy, history and music. These artistic interests have played an important role in his designs.

One Shell Plaza, Houston, Texas (1971)
When completed in 1971, One Shell Plaza was the world's tallest concrete building. The tower's 50 stories extend 714 feet (217.6 m) from the ground. Bruce Graham worked with Fazlur Khan on this building. Like the Sears Tower, Khan used tubes to bring Bruce's design to life. The pair later worked on the plaza's companion building, Two Shell Plaza.

Hotel Arts, Barcelona, Spain (1992)
Bruce Graham partnered with another famous architect, Frank O. Gehry, to design the Hotel Arts in Barcelona. In 1992, the city hosted the Summer Olympics. The hotel was part of the city's Olympic Village. With a height of 505 feet (154 m) and 45 stories, the building towers over the city's waterfront. It is one of Barcelona's leading luxury hotels.

The Science Behind
the Building

When designing and constructing a building, there are many scientific
ideas that have to be taken into account. The architects who design the
buildings have to follow many rules so the buildings will stand strong and
sure. These rules relate to the materials that should be used and the way
these materials are put together.

Carrying the Load

When building a structure, architects and engineers must take into account
the weight of the materials being used. They must determine how they will
affect each other and the land on which the building sits. The building
must be able to withstand its own weight, the weight of the furniture and
equipment inside it, and the forces that may act upon it, such as gravity
and weather.

The bundled tube system used to build the Sears Tower plays a direct role
in **load-bearing**. Prior to the Sears Tower, most buildings handled the
gravity load with columns in the interior of the building. With the bundled
tube system, each tube provides its own support and works with the other
tubes to provide support inside the building and around its edge.

Like concrete, steel is also long-lasting and resistant to wear.

Like the columns, the tubes help the building resist the pull of gravity. The tubes also help the building bear forces that come laterally, or from the side, such as wind. The square shape of the tubes gives the building strength and allows it to stay reasonably still when lateral forces act on it.

Concrete and Steel

A building as big as the Sears Tower needs to be made from strong materials. The two main materials used were concrete and steel.

Concrete makes up the building's **foundation** and its floor slabs. Concrete is known for its strength and its ability to stand up to many of the conditions a building will experience. It takes a long time to show signs of wear, and is resistant to freezing and thawing. It is also watertight. All of these **properties** made it a good material to use in the construction of the Sears Tower. Two million cubic feet (56,634 cubic meters) of concrete were used to build the Sears Tower.

Steel was used for the framework of the Sears Tower. Steel is both strong and lightweight. It provides the support the building needs, but is also easy for workers to handle. Steel can be cut or molded into whatever shape or form the architect needs. This was of great use in building the Sears Tower.

Science and Technology

The construction of a massive building like the Sears Tower takes the efforts of many people. They have to work together to make it a success. People cannot build such a building alone. They need help from machines. Many of the machines used rely on basic principles of science to operate.

Cranes

One of the main challenges in building a tall structure is getting the materials up to the higher levels. This job normally falls to machines called cranes.

Cranes use a simple machine called a pulley to lift and move heavy objects from one place to another. Pulley systems are wheels that have ropes or cables wrapped around them. When an object needs to be moved, it is attached to a hook at one end of the rope or cable. The other end of the rope of cable is then pulled, and the object is lifted. The wheel changes the direction of the force. Applying force to the rope at ground level will lift a load to great heights.

When building the Sears Tower, four cranes were used to move sections of steel into place. They carried the steel higher with each completed floor. It would have been difficult to lift the large sections up the structure without the use of these four cranes.

Pile Drivers

When the foundation for the Sears Tower was being built, workers drove a series of **piles** deep into the ground to provide more support for the building. The piles were forced into the ground using machines called pile drivers. These machines essentially drop weight onto the pile, driving it downwards into the ground. This works like hitting a nail with a hammer. Most pile drivers use a hydraulic system to provide the force needed to get the piles into the ground.

Some cranes can lift as much as 39,690 pounds (18,003 kilograms).

Pile drivers use a pulley system.

A hydraulic system uses two pistons in cylinders filled with an incompressible oil. The oil is pumped to the cylinders and pistons through valves. The pistons are connected by a pipe. When pressure is applied to one piston, the oil transfers the force to the other piston. As one piston is pushed down, the other is lifted by the oil. The pistons move back and forth to power the pile driver.

Portland Cement and Concrete

Concrete was used to build the foundation and the floor slabs of the Sears Tower. Most concrete is made using Portland cement. Portland cement is the ingredient that holds the concrete together.

When making Portland cement, materials such as clay, limestone, and sand are crushed together and poured into a kiln, a type of oven. The heat inside the kiln breaks down the materials so that they form new substances.

Once the materials have been broken down, they are removed from the kiln and mixed with water. The cement then becomes concrete. It is poured into a special truck that has a rotating barrel. The barrel turns constantly in order to keep the concrete from settling and hardening. The truck takes the concrete to the construction site, where it is poured into its mold.

Once poured, the surface of the concrete is kept damp so that it can **cure**. The longer the concrete is allowed to cure, the stronger it will be.

Cement was first used by the Ancient Egyptians nearly 5,000 years ago. They used it to build pyramids.

Quick Bites

- The simplest crane ever built included three pulleys. It was used by the Greeks and the Romans in the late 6th century. This was where and when cranes were first used.
- The concrete used to build the Sears Tower could have built 5 miles (8 km) of an eight-lane highway.

Computer-Aided Design

Architects are trained professionals who work with clients to design structures. Before anything is built, they make detailed drawings or models. These plans are important tools that help people visualize what the structure will look like. A blueprint is a detailed diagram that shows where all the parts of the structure will be placed. Walls, doors, windows, plumbing, electrical wiring, and other details are mapped out on the blueprint. Blueprints act as a guide for engineers and builders during construction.

For centuries, architects and builders worked without the aid of computers. Sketches and blueprints were drawn by hand. Highly skilled drafters would draw very technical designs. Today, this process is done using computers and sophisticated software programs. Architects use CAD, or computer-aided design, throughout the design process. Early CAD systems used computers to draft building plans. Today's computer programs can do much more. They can build three-dimensional models and computer simulations of how a building will look. They can also calculate the effects of different physical forces on the structure. Using CAD, today's architects can build more complex structures at lower cost and in less time.

Computer-aided design programs have been used since the 1960s.

Eye on Design

Placing Antennas Using 3D

The height of the Sears Tower is 1,450 feet (442 m), but the structure's entire height is a little more than 1,730 feet (527 m). This additional height is due to the antennas that sit on top of the skyscraper. They were placed there using CAD's three-dimensional technology.

Antenna are common on many tall structures, such as the Oriental Pearl Tower in China.

Three-dimensional technology is used to provide a 360-degree view of a place. Where two-dimensional technology provides length and width information, 3D gives an image depth as well. This gives planners a good idea of the size and weight of the antenna, as well as a detailed view of the environment in which it will be placed.

In the case of the Sears Tower antennas, planners used computers to create models of the antennas that were to be placed on top of the structure. They used these models to position the antennas properly so that they would pick up signals properly and not interfere with each other's transmissions. From this point, the planners began to figure out how to place the wiring needed to operate each of the antennas. Once they had a detailed model prepared, they moved to assembling the actual antennas on top of the building. In this instance, using CAD saved the planners valuable time as they did not have to experiment with the actual equipment while trying to assemble it.

MEASURING THE SEARS TOWER

Location

The Sears Tower is located on Adams Street and Wacker Drive, in downtown Chicago, Illinois. Wacker Drive is considered one of Chicago's main streets.

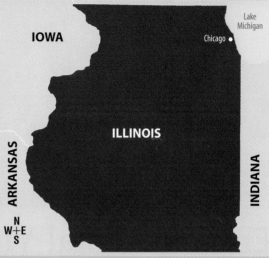

Base

The base of the tower measures approximately 50,625 square feet (4,703 sq m). The building site is equal to 2.96 acres (0.01 sq m).

Weight

The weight of the building has been recorded as 222,500 tons (201,667 tonnes), or 444,600,000 pounds (201,667,168 kilograms).

Other Interesting Facts

- There are six roof-mounted window washing machines to wash the 16,100 windows of the Sears Tower.
- The restrooms on the Skydeck level are considered to be the highest restrooms in the world.
- There are a total of 104 elevators that service the 110 floors of the Sears Tower.

Height

The building itself is 1,450 feet (442 m) above the ground.

In 1982, two television antennas were added to the top of the Sears Tower. These antennas measure 253 feet (77 m) and 283 feet (86 m).

Environmental Viewpoint

Large buildings, merely by their great size, are bound to impact the environment in a negative way. For the past two years, the owners of the Sears Tower have been working to reduce the impact the building has on the environment.

A structure the size of the Sears Tower uses a great deal of electricity. This use can put a strain on the community and its environment. The Sears Tower now voluntarily reduces the energy it uses at times when electricity is in demand. The owners have also started looking at some of the systems that operate within the building. Plans are already underway to improve the tower's **insulation** and change the type of lighting the building uses. Both of these changes will help the structure control its use of power. The insulation will keep the Sears Tower warmer in cold weather, which will reduce the amount of heat the building needs. By changing the lighting to something more **eco-friendly**, the tower will also use less electricity.

This eco-friendly **retrofit** will help to make sure that the community has the power it needs and avoid having to increase the amount of power created at local power plants. Many of the plants produce **greenhouse gases** when generating power. Controlling the amount of power needed helps reduce greenhouse gases.

The environment is important to the people who operate the Sears Tower. In 2008, the Sears Tower started a courtesy bike program for tenants. During the week, tenants can borrow a bicycle for to use at no charge. This helps reduce traffic and gas emissions in Chicago.

A GREEN ROOF

Part of the planned retrofit of the Sears Tower includes the creation of a "green" roof. A green roof is the roof of a building that is partially or entirely covered in vegetation and soil. These roofs are environmentally friendly because they help to keep the building cool in the summers and warm in the winters.

Green roofs also assist in reducing storm water runoff. When there is a big rainstorm, the greenery absorbs the water and uses it to grow. Without a green roof, the water would run off the building and into the streets. It would then flow into the water system, carrying with it all the **pollutants** it picked up along the way. This makes water, a very limited resource, unsafe for animals, including people and plants.

Green roofs help to filter out pollutants in the air. The plants absorb carbon dioxide and produce breathable air.

Construction Careers

Building a structure the size of the Sears Tower requires a large team of people. Architects, engineers, steelworkers, crane operators, electricians, and many others played an important role in the construction of the Sears Tower. The construction process faced its share of challenges, but everyone involved used their knowledge, skills, and experience to find solutions to problems.

Architect

Architects design buildings and the spaces around them. They sometimes have a team working with them, helping them in planning the construction of a building. It is their job to manage this team responsibly. An architect's building decisions are based on the safety and well-being of people. The architect must also consider the needs of the person or company that is paying for the building. Both the public and the client have many needs

that must be met. Architects must be able to communicate their plans and the reasons for them to all parties involved in the project. An architect should be creative and have the technical knowledge needed to produce buildings that are functional yet attractive in appearance.

Structural Engineer

Structural engineers study the architect's design and work out the details needed to bring the design into reality. Their job relies mainly on a knowledge of science principles involved in carrying loads. The structural engineer makes sure that the building will hold together under its weight, the weight of everything in it, and the forces that work against it. They inspect the building at different stages of the building process to make sure the structure can withstand forces, such as wind, rain, and vibration. Engineers are people who develop safe and cost-effective ways of solving problems. A structural engineer most commonly designs buildings and other large structures but can also work on machinery, vehicles, medical equipment, and other items.

Concrete Finishers

Construction workers that specialize in concrete are called concrete finishers. They work both indoors and out, depending on the task. Concrete finishers pour wet concrete into casts and spread it to a desired thickness. They level and smooth the surface and edges of the concrete. Concrete finishers also repair, waterproof, and restore concrete surfaces. A concrete finisher's work is very physical and often involves lifting heavy bags of cement, bending and kneeling.

Web Link:
To find out more about construction careers, visit
www.constructmyfuture.com

Notable Structures

Since the building of the Sears Tower, even higher buildings have been constructed. The Sears Tower, once the world's tallest building, is now ranked as the fourth highest building in the world. It may not be long before it drops farther down in the rankings.

Burj Dubai

Built: 2009

Location: Dubai, United Arab Emirates

Architect: Skidmore, Owings, & Merrill

Description: When it is completed in the fall of 2009, the Burj Dubai will be the world's newest tallest building. It will be 2,684 feet (818 m) tall and have 162 floors. The first 37 floors will house a hotel. The middle floors have been set aside for apartment space. The top 52 floors will be mainly office space.

Taipei 101

Built: 2004

Location: Taipei, Taiwan

Architect: CY Lee & Partners

Description: Taipei 101 is currently the world's tallest completed building. It reaches a height of 1,671 feet (509 m) and has 101 stories aboveground and another five floors underground. In 2006, it was named one of the Seven New Wonders of the World.

Around the world, people continue to plan the construction of tall buildings, with each hoping to build a structure that will become as well-known as the United States' Sears Tower.

Shanghai World Financial Center

Built: 2008

Location: Shanghai, China

Design: Kohn Pedersen Fox

Description: With 101 floors and a height of 1,614 feet (492 m), the Shanghai World Financial Center is currently the world's second tallest building. The center is easily recognized by the opening at the top of the structure. Designed to help fight wind forces, the hole gives the building a bottle-opener appearance.

Petronas Towers

Built: 1998

Location: Kuala Lumpur, Malaysia

Design: Cesar Pelli

Description: Both of the Petronas Towers rise to a height of 1,483 (452 m). The design of the towers was inspired by the art of a religion called Islam. Although they look identical, the two towers were built by two different construction companies. The companies competed to see who could raise their tower the fastest.

Skyscrapers Around the World

A skyscraper is defined as a building that rises above a city's skyline, giving it a distinctive appearance. Skyscrapers can be found in many parts of the world.

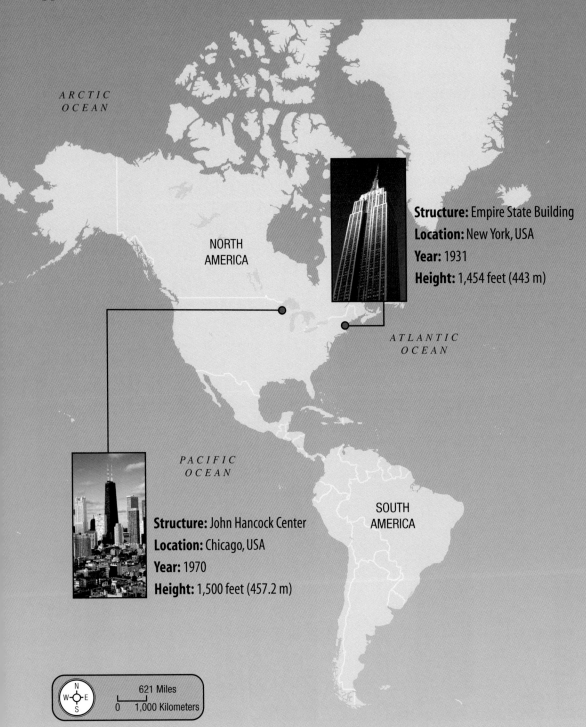

ARCTIC
OCEAN

NORTH
AMERICA

Structure: Empire State Building
Location: New York, USA
Year: 1931
Height: 1,454 feet (443 m)

ATLANTIC
OCEAN

PACIFIC
OCEAN

Structure: John Hancock Center
Location: Chicago, USA
Year: 1970
Height: 1,500 feet (457.2 m)

SOUTH
AMERICA

621 Miles
0   1,000 Kilometers

Not all of them can rank as the tallest in the world. Still, they contribute to the city in which they stand and become landmarks in their own right.

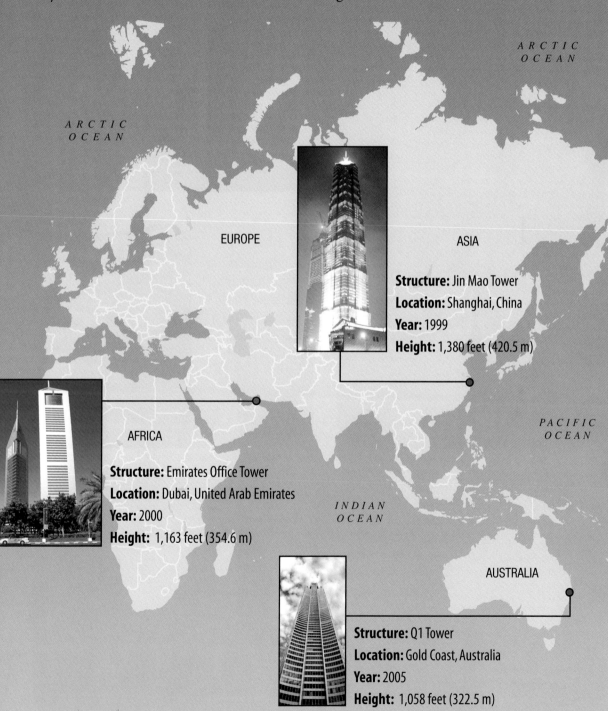

ARCTIC
OCEAN

ARCTIC
OCEAN

EUROPE

ASIA

Structure: Jin Mao Tower
Location: Shanghai, China
Year: 1999
Height: 1,380 feet (420.5 m)

PACIFIC
OCEAN

AFRICA

Structure: Emirates Office Tower
Location: Dubai, United Arab Emirates
Year: 2000
Height: 1,163 feet (354.6 m)

INDIAN
OCEAN

AUSTRALIA

Structure: Q1 Tower
Location: Gold Coast, Australia
Year: 2005
Height: 1,058 feet (322.5 m)

Quiz

Q Who was the main architect of the Sears Tower?

A Bruce Graham

S WACKER DR

Q Who was Fazlur Khan?

A He was the chief structural engineer for the Sears Tower.

Q What structural design technique did Fazlur Khan develop for the Sears Tower?

A Bundled tubes to provide the structure's support

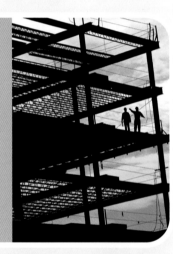

Q How tall is the Sears Tower?

A 1,450 feet (442 m) without antennas; more than 1,730 feet (527 m) with antennas

Build a Bundled-tube Tower

The Sears Tower was the first building to use bundled tubes to handle gravity and wind loads. Due to the success of this building style, other buildings have been built using this technique. Test the strength and stability of the bundled tube system by building your own tower.

Materials
• yard or meter stick
• newspaper
• scissors
• scotch tape

Instructions
1. Decide how tall your tower will be and how many tubes will be needed to make it, keeping in mind that it must be sturdy enough to resist wind loads.

2. Using the yard or meter stick, cut the sheets of newspapers to the size you want each tube to be.

3. Roll each sheet into a tube.

4. Tape or tie the tubes together to form your tower.

5. Stand about an arm's length away from your tower, and blow with all your might. Did your building topple over or stay upright? What do you think caused it to do so?

Further Research

There is a great deal of information on the Internet about the Sears Tower and other tall buildings around the world. You can also search your local library for information.

Websites

For more information about the Sears Tower, visit
www.searstower.com

To read more about Fazlur Khan, visit
www.fazlurrkhan.com

For a history of the world's tallest buildings, visit
www.skyscraper.org

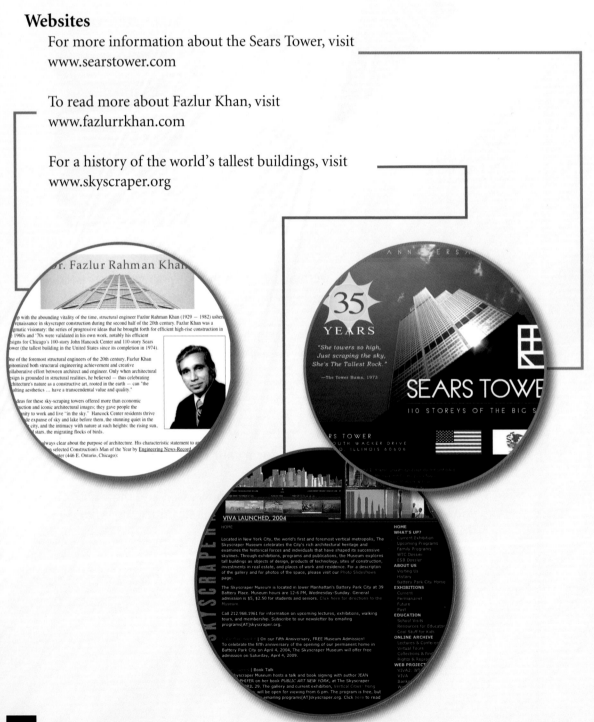

Glossary

architect: a person who designs buildings

beam: a horizontal support

cladding: the bonding of one metal to another to form a protective coating

columns: vertical supports

cure: to harden a material, especially concrete or cement

eco-friendly: good for the environment

facade: the front of a building

foundation: the base on which something stands

greenhouse gases: gases that are making Earth warm

groundbreaking ceremony: an event in which someone digs up dirt as a beginning to a building's construction

insulation: a material used to keep a building at constant temperature

landmark: a well-known object in a specific location

load-bearing: the ability of something to hold up against a weight or force

piles: columns that are driven into the ground to support a vertical load

pollutants: substances that make something unhealthy

properties: qualities or attributes

retrofit: to equip something with new parts

stories: the floors or levels of a building

structural engineer: a person who applies the principles of science and mathematics to the building of a structure

topping out ceremony: an event that represents the placement of the highest beam on a building

Index